PEPSI-COLA

COLLECTIBLES

Vol. 3

(with prices)

For Additional Books
Order From

L-W BOOK SALES

Box 69
Gas City, IN 46933

© 1993
Bill Vehling
Michael Hunt

2nd Printing 1994

A

TABLE OF CONTENTS

PREFACE

Well folks, here we are again, composing the introduction to our third book. Believe us when we tell you, this is the last one!!!! It is the last, but hopefully it is the best. We have a large amount of rare pieces never before published or seen. We have also added to this volume an extensive color section which we feel will enhance your enjoyment of the book.

Just a word or two about the color section – in volume two, we made it a point not to put in any pieces that were in volume one. We have done this again for volume three, except in the color section. We felt that they deserved to be shown in color and hope our readers feel the same way. Each piece in the color section is also shown in its appropriate black and white section, along with its value, description, size, and date.

When we wrote our first book in 1986, the membership of the Pepsi Cola Collectors Club (P C C C) was less than five hundred. Now it is over two thousand! That is quite an increase in seven years. With this increase in the number of collectors, the demand for quality pieces has also increased. With increased demand comes increased prices. We will discuss prices later. In the same time period, Pepsi Fest, Pepsi Fest West, advertising and collectibles shows, auctions, antique malls, etc., have burst upon the scene and have flourished. These have afforded the collector numerous places to find that elusive Pepsi piece he or she is lusting for. We constantly hear comments from collectors who say "We can't afford the prices there", or "It wouldn't be worth our time to go there" or "We would get blown away by the collectors there". Well, we say this just isn't so. In late 1992 in Virginia, there was an auction of one of the oldest and nicest collections of Pepsi pieces ever assembled. At this auction there were numerous rare or possibly "one-of-a-kind" items that sold for ridiculously low prices. Things like this are happening all the time. If this had been a collection of Coca Cola pieces of the same age, quality, and rarity, there would have been hundreds of avid bidders there. At this auction, there were barely over one hundred. Prices in this auction ranged, in our opinion, from reasonable to cheap. Many bargains were there for the taking. At comparable Coca Cola or quality antique advertising auctions, these types of pieces would bring five to ten times the money that these brought. So, why don't all you "serious" Pepsi collectors get out there and get some of these bargains before the Coke collectors start buying them up because they can't afford Coke stuff anymore!!!!

Now we must address the "method of our madness" in pricing items in this book. We, being dealers in antique advertising, have priced these items as we would have comparable Coke items, advertising tins, or advertising signs. That is to say, why shouldn't the earliest known Pepsi calendar or tray be comparable in value to the earliest Coke calendar or tray? or the rarest tobacco or coffee tin? or the earliest or rarest tin advertising sign? We think they should be and this book, as were our others, is priced in this manner. Why should a 1960's light-up sign sell for considerably more than a "one-of-a-kind" artist's painting of a 1930's Pepsi bottling plant, or more than a rare 1913 calendar, or more than a vintage 1910 cardboard sign? In our opinion, it should not! It is our opinion that the fraternity of Pepsi collectors for the most part, not totally, are not giving the appreciation to the rare and vintage pieces, monetarily, that they deserve. A pocket mirror collector is offering to buy as many Gibson Girl Pepsi mirrors as he can for $5000 each. A soda can collector is offering to pay $1000 for the five bottle-cap cone top can. A few years back, a doctor paid $9500 for the ceramic syrup dispenser because "his wife would like the flowers on it." A double-domed clock collector will pay up to $500 for a 1950's clock with bottle caps for numbers. A neon collector paid nearly $5000 for a Pepsi neon clock. These are the facts. The facts are that non-Pepsi collectors are getting these top-flight pieces because they are willing to pay the asking price or more for them. If other collectors are willing to pay these prices, then why won't the true Pepsi collector? We wish we knew the answer. We certainly do not wish to offend any collector, and if we have done so, we profusely apologize. Being that this is our last book, we wanted to hop up on our soapbox. We are not trying to criticize the collector, but we are instead trying to open their eyes and advise them that early, quality, rare, and aesthetic pieces are limited in numbers and are disappearing into collections every day. Look at your collection as an investment as well as what appeals to you. It's better than money in the bank! Remember, that nasty old Coke collector is out there lurking.

We must, in all honesty, note that many of our prices in this book are too low. Certain categories of Pepsi pieces are escalating in price and demand so fast that we can't keep up. Items such as 1930's and 1940's cardboard (Pepsi and Pete and self-framed girls), lighted clocks of the 1950's and 1960's, and lighted signs are selling for astronomical amounts. We have tried to be as fair and accurate as we can in all our pricing. We are trying, not only to give our readers a general idea of the values of pieces they might be wishing to buy, but also we are trying to give the collector an idea as to the value of his or her collection. We feel it would be a travesty if we priced our book according to what we wanted to pay for these pieces. Oh, wait a minute you say, you are dealers who sell these pieces and your prices are high because you want to sell them for a lot of money. Our prices are based on current market values, either through personal sales, auction sales, other dealer's sales, or collector's sales. Remember, as we have said before, this book is only meant to be a GUIDE! Actual values are what the seller wants to sell it for and what the buyer wants to pay.

In regards to new items: you will not find any in this book. Nearly all pieces herein are pre-1970. In book two, we made a big mistake by including a section on new items. Our field of expertise in Pepsi collectibles is 1900's-1960's. There are thousands of Pepsi items out there produced in the 1970's and 1980's. We are not knowledgeable when it comes to value or rarity of these types of items. We will leave that to other authors. As we stated before, collecting can be two-fold. If you enjoy collecting the newer items, more power to you. If you are collecting as an investment, then please focus your buying toward the older items. End of commentary.

We have enjoyed over the past seven years corresponding with fellow collectors and we will still do so in the future regarding unique Pepsi pieces you have run across.

We have appreciated your support over the years and hope that you will continue to give us that same support in the future. We know we can't please everyone, but we sincerely hope our books have helped to make Pepsi collecting more enjoyable to everyone.

ACKNOWLEDGEMENTS

Putting together a book requires a lot of help from a lot of people. We wish to thank the following friends and collectors without whose help this book would not have been possible.

Gary Craig

Marty Weinberger

Mary Lloyd

Gary Metz-Muddy River Trading Co.

Sterling and Margaret Mann

With special thanks to . . .

Jay and Joan Millman –   Our special friends who once again opened their new home in Pennsylvania to us and allowed us to photograph the new additions to their fine collection.

Terry and Martha Lunt –   Friends who provided us with numerous photos of their extensive collection.

Allan Petretti –   Fellow author who again provided us with several photos.

Scott and Kim Kinzie –   Who opened their home and fine collection to us.

Neil Wood –   Our long time friend and terrific publisher without whose assistance none of our books would have been possible.

E

DATING, GRADING AND SIZING

Dating   If items were dated they are noted as such. We have tried to date all other pieces within ten years and these are noted with the word "circa".

Sizing   We have attempted to give accurate sizes whenever possible. Sizes are given as follows:

Width
Height
Depth

When only one dimension is given, it refers to length.

Grading   BE CONSERVATIVE! The owner of an item, whether he is a collector or a dealer, tends to over-grade his particular item. Don't Fool Yourself!

Main factors in determining condition:

Metal items – fading or discoloration of paint, chips, scratches, dents, or rust.

Paper or cardboard items – tears, waterspotting or other discoloration.

China or glass items – chips or cracks.

For all pieces in general be sure they have no missing parts and have not been restored. Restoration, if done properly, in most cases will make the item appear more presentable but it will not be "original". It should be left to the buyer and/or owner as to whether he prefers the piece to be "original" or restored.

ABOUT THE AUTHORS

Michael Hunt, a life-long resident of Indiana, has been in the antique business for 25 years. The last 12 years have been devoted full time to the business, enabling he and his wife, Sharon, to travel extensively buying, selling, and visiting other collectors across the country.

Michael and Sharon collect a wide range of antique advertising including Pepsi Cola items. They are members of Pepsi Cola Collectors Club (PCCC), Antique Advertising Association of America (AAAA) and Tin Containers Collectors Association (TCCA).

Bill Vehling has been collecting, buying and selling antique advertising since 1975. He has specialized in soda water related advertising, especially Pepsi Cola. He and his wife, Amy, travel extensively on week-ends and during the summer months to shows and auctions seeking those elusive pieces to add to their collection or for resale.

The Vehlings are members of the Pepsi Cola Collectors Club (PCCC), Antique Advertising Association of America (AAAA), The Coca Cola Collectors Club, and the Tin Container Collectors Association (TCCA).

When wishing either of them to reply to a question, please send a SASE to:

Bill Vehling
P.O. Box 42233
Indianapolis, IN 46242

Michael Hunt
P.O. Box 546
Brownsburg, IN 46112

#1
Enameled Service Pin
Circa 1900's
1" x 1"
$600

#2
Gold Bottle with enameled inlay
Circa 1930's
3" x 10"
$500

#3
Volume Award (Durham, N.C.)
1953 – 12" x 12"
$75

#4
Per Capita Award (Durham, N.C.)
1953 – 12" x 12"
$75

AWARDS

#5
Racing Trophy
1962 – 32"
$275

#6
Trophy
1974 – 12" Diameter
$75

#7
Salesman of the Month Plaque
1969 – 12" x 16"
$50

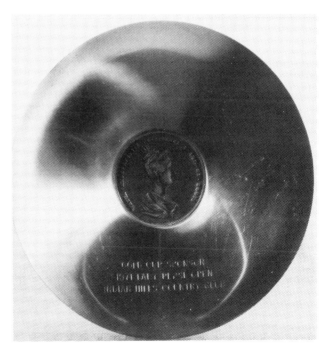

#8
Platter (Pepsi Golf Tourney)
1971 – 12"
$25

BOTTLE CARRIERS

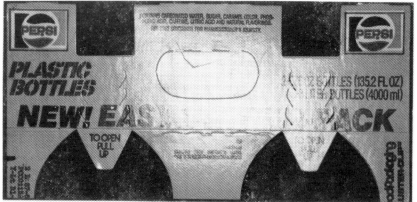

#9
Cardboard (2 liter plastic bottle carrier)
Circa 1970's
2 Bottles
$10

#10
Cardboard case
Circa 1960's
24 Bottles
$25

#11
Cardboard case
Circa 1960's
24 Bottles
$25

#12
Paper Bottle Bag
Circa 1940's
6 Bottles
$125

#13
Cardboard case
Circa 1950's
12 Bottles
$75

#14
Cardboard case
Circa 1950's
24 Bottles
$50

BOTTLE CARRIERS

#15
Cardboard
Circa 1960's
2 Bottles
$75

#16
Cardboard
Circa 1960's
6 Cans
$25

#17
Cardboard
Circa 1960's
6 Bottles
$25

#18
Cardboard
Circa 1950's
12 Bottles
$35

#19
Wooden Case
Circa 1940's
24 Bottles
$75

BOTTLE CARRIERS

#20
Cardboard Carton (Patio)
Circa 1960's
6 Bottles
$25

#21
Cardboard Carton
(Mountain Dew)
Circa 1960's
6 Bottles
$25

#22
Cardboard Six-Pack
(Evervess)
Circa 1940's
6 Bottles
$25

#25
Cardboard Carton
Circa 1960's
6 Bottles
$15

#23
Cloth Bag
Circa 1940's
8" x 6"
$75

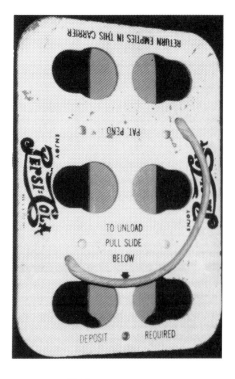

#24
Composition (6 Bottles)
Circa 1940's
12" x 6"
$150

BOTTLE CARRIERS

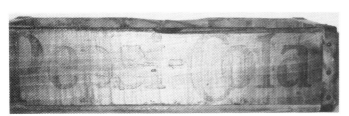

#26
Wooden Case
Circa 1910's
24 Bottle
$125

#27
Wooden Crate (72 Bottles)
(Rawleigh, N.C.)
1908 – 36" x 10 1/2" x 18"
$450

#28
Wooden Crate (72 Bottles)
(Charlottesville, VA)
1908
36" x 10 1/2" x 18"
$450

#29
Wooden Case
Circa 1910's
24 Bottles
$150

#30
Wooden Case (Canadian)
Circa 1930's
24 Bottles
$125

#31
Wooden Case
Circa 1910's
24 Bottles
$200

BOTTLE CARRIERS

#32
Metal
Circa 1940's
6 Bottles
$100

#33
Wooden Six-Pack
Circa 1930's
8" x 9"
$175

#34
Metal Carrier
Circa 1930's
6 Bottles
$150

#35
Metal Twelve-Pack
Circa 1940's
12 Bottles
$250

#36
Metal
Circa 1930's
6 Bottles
$150

BOTTLE OPENERS

#37
Opener / Spoon
Circa 1910's
10"
$150

#38
Opener with spoon
Circa 1910's
8"
$150

#39
Opener with Spoon (Waco, Texas)
Circa 1910's
8"
$150

#40
Opener with original mailer
2"
$75

BOTTLE OPENERS

#41
Plastic Handle
Circa 1940's
6"
$50

#42
Plastic Handle
Circa 1950's
4"
#35

#43
Plastic Handle
Circa 1950's
6"
$25

#44
Plastic Handle
Circa 1960's
6"
$25

#45
Plastic Handle
Circa 1960's
6"
$25

BOTTLE OPENERS

#46
Metal Opener
Circa 1950's
4"
$25

#47
Tin (Over-The-Top)
Circa 1950's
4"
$35

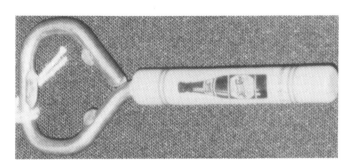

#48
Celluloid Handle
Circa 1930's
4"
$150

#49
Metal (Quincy, IL)
Circa 1930's
3" x 1 1/2"
$150

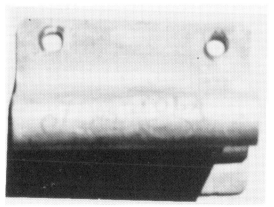

#50
Wall Opener
Circa 1920's
2" x 2"
$125

#51
Etched Seltzer
Bottle (Clear)
Jacksonville, FL
Circa 1910
36 oz.
$800

#52
Etched Seltzer Bottle (Amber)
Jacksonville, FL
Circa 1910
36 oz.
$1000

#54
Diet Pepsi
(Throw Away)
Circa 1960's
10 oz.
$25

#53
Applied Color Label
Circa 1960's
32 oz.
$50

#55
Paper Label No Return
Circa 1960's
29 oz.
$100

BOTTLES

#56
Embossed (No Return)
Circa 1950's
6 oz.
$125

#57
Embossed (No Return)
Circa 1940's
6 oz.
$250

#58
Applied Color Label
Circa 1960's
32 oz. (No Deposit)
$75

#59
Embossed (No Return)
Circa 1950's
8 oz.
$125

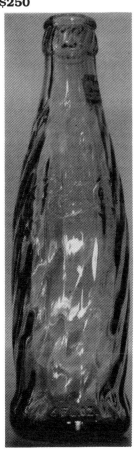

#60
Pink Prototype
(Wheaton Glass Co.)
1953 – 6 oz.
$550

#61
Throwaway
Circa 1950's
8 oz.
$125

BOTTLES

#62
Applied Color Label
Circa 1960's
28 oz.
$100

#63
Plastic Throwaway
Circa 1960's
16 oz.
$10

#64
Paper Label
Circa 1950's
26 oz.
$150

#65
Foil Label
Circa 1950's
32 oz.
$150

#66
Applied Color Label
(Mexican)
Circa 1940's
12 oz.
$35

#67
Mini Bottle
(Paper Label)
Circa 1940's
3"
$75

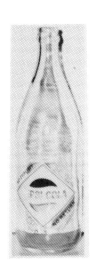

#68
Applied Color Label
Throwaway – 1967
26 oz.
$100

#69
Paper Label
(No Return)
Circa 1950's
26 oz.
$125

BOTTLES

#70
Throwaway
Circa 1960's
16 oz.
$10

#71
Indian Rock
Richmond, VA
(Clear) – 6 1/2 oz.
$600

#72
Throwaway
Circa 1960's
10 oz.
$10

#73
Throwaway
Circa 1960's
10 oz.
$10

#74
Jacksonville, FL (Clear)
Circa 1910's
6 1/2 oz.
$200

#75
Throwaway
Circa 1960's
12 oz.
$15

#76
Throwaway
Circa 1960's
16 oz.
$10

#77
Throwaway
Circa 1960's
10 oz.
$10

#78
Throwaway
Circa 1960's
16 oz.
$10

BOTTLES

#79
Lexington, VA
(Green)
Circa 1910's
6 1/2 oz.
$125

#80
Lynchburg, VA
(Green)
Circa 1910's
6 1/2 oz.
$200

#81
Norfolk, VA
(Green)
Circa 1910's
6 1/2 oz.
$125

#82
Suffolk, VA (Green)
Circa 1910's
6 1/2 oz.
$125

#83
Richmond, VA
(Green) 8 Side
Circa 1910's
6 1/2 oz.
$300

#84
Jessup Bottling Works
Charlottesville, VA
Circa 1910's
6 1/2 oz.
$200

#85
Richmond, VA
(Clear)
Circa 1910's
6 1/2 oz.
$200

#86
Newport News, VA
(Clear)
Circa 1910's
6 1/2 oz.
$200

#87
Newport News, VA
(Clear)
Circa 1910's
6 1/2 oz.
$150

BOTTLES

#88
Applied Color Label
Circa 1960's
10 oz.
$75

#89
Applied Color Label
Circa 1960's
7 oz.
$10

#90
Applied Color Label
Circa 1960's
8 oz.
$10

#91
Rock Creek
Circa 1930's
24 oz.
$150

#92
Applied Color Label
Circa 1960's
10 oz.
$10

#93
Applied Color Label
Circa 1960's
10 oz.
$10

#94
Norfolk, VA – Amber
Circa 1910's
7 oz.
$250

#95
Memphis, TN – Amber
Circa 1910's
6 1/2 oz.
$200

#96
Amber Throwaway
Circa 1960's
6 oz.
$75

#97
Paper Label
Circa 1940's
12 oz.
$75

#98
Richmond, VA – Clear
Circa 1910's
6 1/2 oz.
$125

#99
Embossed No Return
Circa 1950's
8 oz.
$125

BOTTLES

#100
Applied Color Label
Circa 1960's
12 oz.
$10

#101
Applied Color Label
Circa 1960's
7 oz.
$10

#102
Paper Label
(Green Glass)
Circa 1950's
28 oz.
$100

#103
Sunny Brook (Suffolk, VA)
Circa 1930's
9 oz.
$200

#104
Sunny Brook (Suffolk, VA)
Circa 1930's
9 oz.
$200

#105
Big Bill (Suffolk, VA)
Circa 1930's
9 oz.
$200

CALENDARS

Top View – Closed

#106
Twelve sheets with cover sheet
1951
10" diameter
$450

#107
Cardboard with
Replaceable Pad
1942
9" x 12"
$650

Top View – Closed

#108
Calendar / Bottle Hanger
1953
4" x 6"
$75

CALENDARS

#109
Tin with Paper Sheets
Circa 1960's
8" x 12"
$35

#110
Cardstock Calendar
1955
12" x 20"
$450

#111
Foil Covered Cardboard
1966
12" x 3"
$25

#112
Cardboard
1967
9" x 15"
$25

#113
Cardboard with
Replaceable Pad
1951 (1940's Logo)
12" x 20"
$600

CALENDARS

#114
Paper with
Twelve Month Pad
1951 (1940's Logo)
15 1/2" x 33"
$650

#115
Paper with
Twelve Month Pad
1950 (1940's Logo)
11" x 24"
$650

#116
Ada Okla. Bottling Co.
1952
6" x 10 1/2"
$300

#117
Heavy Paper
Twelve Month Pad
1960 (1940's Logo)
16" x 33"
$750

CALENDARS

#118
Heavy Paper with
Twelve Month Pad
1910
10" x 19"
$3800

#119
Heavy Paper with
Twelve Month Pad
1909
10" x 19"
$3800

#120
Heavy Paper
Twelve Month Pad
1913
12" x 19"
$4500

#121
"The Pepsi Cola Girl"
(R. Armstrong Art)
1921
14" x 25"
$3500

#122
Cardboard with
Twelve Month Pad
1939
7" x 14"
$900

#123
Two Double Sheets
1953
11 1/2" x 17 1/2"
$275

#124
Foil Cardboard with
Plastic Bottles
1968
19" x 11"
$175

#125
Heavy Paper
1965
14" x 18"
$50

CALENDARS

#126
Four Sheet (Mexican)
1966
14" x 20"
$75

#127
Cardboard
1952
9" x 16"
$400

#128
Paper with
Twelve Month Pad
1962 (1940's Logo)
11" x 23"
$750

#129
Cardboard (R. Armstrong Art)
1920
5" x 7"
$4800

CANS

#130
Steel Pull Tab
Circa 1960's
9 1/2 oz.
$25

#131
Steel Pull Tab
Circa 1960's
10 oz.
$25

#132
Steel Pull Tab
Circa 1960's
9 1/2 oz.
$25

#133
Steel Pull-Tab
Circa 1960's
12 oz.
$25

#134
Steel
Circa 1960's
12 oz.
$35

#135
Steel Pull Tab
Circa 1960's
12 oz.
$50

#136
Pull Tab Can
Circa 1960's
12 oz.
$25

#137
Aluminum
Circa 1960's
12 oz.
$25

#138
Steel Cone Top
Circa 1940's
12 oz.
$750

#139
Bicentennial
Cone Top
1976
12 oz.
$20

#140
Aluminum
(Resealable)
Circa 1970's
1/2 Liter
$25

#141
Aluminum
(Resealable)
Circa 1970's
1/2 Liter
$25

CLOCKS

#142
Plastic Counter Clock
Circa 1970's
14" x 6"
$50

#143
Double-Domed Glass
(Lighted)
Circa 1950's
16" Diameter
$350

#144
Plastic and Metal
Circa 1960's
18" Diameter
$275

#145
Glass Front Lighted
Circa 1960's
16" x 16"
$175

#146
Neon with Reverse Glass Race
Circa 12" x 16"
12" x 16"
$6000

#147
Plastic
Circa 1970's
14" Diameter
$150

CLOCKS

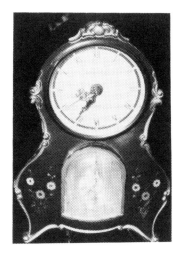

#148
Animated Windup
(Red Case)
Circa 1920's
4" x 6"
$1250

#150
Double Tube Neon with
Reverse Glass Sign
Circa 1930's
24" x 24"
$9000

#149
Animated Windup (White Case)
Circa 1920's
4" x 6"
$1250

#151
Glass Light-Up
Circa 1940's
15" Diameter
$425

#152
Plastic Front Neon Tube
Circa 1950's
30" Diameter
$1000

CLOCKS

#153
Light-up
Circa 1950's
30"
$350

#154
Tin Face / Glass Cover
Circa 1950's
16" x 16"
$275

#155
Plastic and Metal
Circa 1960's
18" Diameter
$250

#156
Plastic Lite-up
Circa 1970's
36" x 36"
$75

#157
Plastic Light-up (Metal Frame)
Circa 1960's
16" x 16"
$225

#158
Plastic/Glass Light-up
Circa 1960's
16" x 16"
$150

#159
Glass Front Light-up
Circa 1950's
20" Diameter
$425

#160
Plastic Light-up
Circa 1960's
18" x 12"
$125

CLOCKS

#161
Glass Light-up
Circa 1950's
15" Diameter
$650

#162
Plastic Lighted
Circa 1950's
17" Diameter
$450

#163
Neon
Circa 1930's
18" x 18"
$2200

CLOCKS

#164
Plastic with Calendar Holder
Circa 1950's
12" Diameter
$325

#165
Moulded Plastic
Circa 1970's
14" Diameter
$50

#166
Neon
Circa 1940's
18" Diameter
$2200

#167
Tin Face
Circa 1950's
16" Diameter
$525

CLOTHING

#168
Plastic Rain Hat
Circa 1950's
$25

#169
Cloth Necktie
Circa 1950's
4" Wide
$50

#170
Laboratory Coat
Circa 1930's
$200

#171
Cloth Vendors Hat
Circa 1940's
$150

#172
Paper Vendors Hat
Circa 1940's
12" x 5"
$50

CLOTHING

#173
Oil Cloth Vendors Hat
Circa 1930's
12" x 6"
$150

#174
Coolie Hat
Circa 1940's
24" Diameter
$75

#175
Cloth Apron
Circa 1930's
18" x 28"
$350

#176
Driver's Hat
Circa 1950's
$75

#177
Pepsi and Pete
(Full Color)
1940
12" x 9"
$35

#178
Pepsi and Pete
(Full Color)
1940
12" x 9"
$35

#179
Pepsi and Pete
(Full Color)
1940
12" x 9"
$35

#180
Pepsi and Pete
(Full Color)
1940
12" x 9"
$35

#181
Pepsi and Pete
(Full Color)
1940
12" x 9"
$35

COOLERS

#182
Closed End Style
Circa 1940's
Single Case
$850

#183
Picnic Cooler / Minnow Bucket
(2 Views)
Circa 1950's
12" x 16" x 12"
$150

#184
Picnic Cooler
Circa 1950's
24" x 16" x 12"
$85

#185
Glasscock Style
Circa 1930's
2 Case
$600

#186
Closed End Style
Circa 1940's – Double Case
$500

COOLERS

#187
Picnic Cooler
Circa 1940's
16" x 24" x 16"
$150

#188
Metal Picnic with Original Box
Circa 1960's
24" x 18" x 14"
$175

#189
Vinyl with Opener
Circa 1950's
Two Bottles
$75

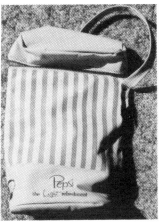

#190
Vinyl Picnic Cooler
Circa 1950's
8" x 12"
$100

#191
Wooden
Circa 1900's
30" x 36"
$500

#192
Wooden and Plastic
Circa 1970's
36" x 40"
$25

COOLERS

#193
Metal Picnic
Circa 1950's
18" x 14" x 12"
$100

#194
Metal Picnic
Circa 1940's
18" x 12" x 9"
$150

#195
Paper Cooler
1980's
12" x 28"
$10

#196
Picnic
Circa 1950's
20" x 14" x 12"
$100

#197
Metal Picnic
Circa 1960's
18" x 14" x 12"
$75

COUPONS

#198
Bottle Deposit Ticket
Circa 1940's
2" x 1 1/2"
$50

#199
Fold-Over
Circa 1940's
6" x 7"
$75

#200
Paper (Two Views)
Circa 1930's
6" x 3"
$100

#201
Fold-Over
Circa 1940's
6" x 7"
$75

#202
Macon, GA
Circa 1940's
5" x 2 1/2"
$50

#203
Circus Ticket
Circa 1930's
5" x 3"
$50

COUPONS

#204
Sno-Ball
Circa 1960's
6" x 4"
$10

#207
Heavy Paper
(Dossins Btlg. Co.)
(Two Views)
Circa 1940's
4" x 2"
$50

#211
Heavy Paper
(2-Views)
Cincinnati, OH
Circa 1930's
3" x 1 1/2"
$75

#205
Tin Token (Ft. Worth, TX)
(Two Views)
Circa 1950's
1" Diameter
$25

#206
Heavy Paper
1910
3" x 1 1/2"
$600

#208
Five Cents
Circa 1950's
3" x 2"
$25

#209
Heavy Paper
Circa 1940's
3" x 1"
$50

#210
Heavy Paper
Circa 1920's
2" x 1"
$75

#212
One Drink Coupon
Circa 1900
3" x 1 1/2"
$600

#213
Paper Cup (Two Views)
Circa 1930's
12 oz.
$175

#214
Applied Color Label
Circa 1950's
10 oz.
$35

#215
Paper Cup
Circa 1930's
12 oz.
$75

#216
Cardboard Cup
Circa 1960's
12 oz.
$10

#217
Cardboard Cup
Circa 1960's
6 oz.
$10

#218
Applied Color Label
Circa 1960's
12 oz.
$35

#219
Convention Glass
1972
10 oz.
$25

#220
Glass
(Birmingham, AL)
1971
10 oz.
$25

#221
Paper Cup
Circa 1950's
6 oz.
$25

#222
Cardboard Box and Glasses
Circa 1950's
Size (12) 10 oz. Glasses
$100

#223
Paper Cup
(Two Views)
Circa 1930's
14 oz.
$75

DESK ITEMS

#224
Metal Paperweight
(Gold Color)
Circa 1970's
3 1/2" Diameter
$15

#225
Metal Paperweight
(Bronze Color)
Circa 1970
3 1/2" Diameter
$15

#226
Metal Paperweight
(Silver Color)
Circa 1970's
3 1/2" Diameter
$15

#227
Plastic Sno-Dome Paperweight
Circa 1960's
3" Diameter
$75

#228
Plastic Bill Holder
(Turtle Shaped)
Circa 1950's
2" x 3"
$25

#229
Paperweight
Circa 1940's
3" x 3"
$100

#230
Paperweight
Circa 1940's
5" x 2"
$100

#231
Notepad Holder
Circa 1960's
4" x 6"
$25

#232
Lucite Paperweight
Circa 1950's
3" x 3" x 3"
$50

#233
Desk Calendar with Mirror
Circa 1950's
2" x 3"
$100

DISPLAYS

#234
Inaugural Can (China)
1982
4" x 9"
$75

#236
Paper
Circa 1980's
12" x 12"
$25

#235
Plastic (Rotates)
Circa 1980's
9" x 6" x 5"
$50

#237
Cardboard
Circa 1970's
18" Diameter
$25

#238
Cardboard (Rotating)
Circa 1970's
4'
$75

DISPLAYS

#239
Tin Straw Holder
Circa 1909
3" x 3" x 6"
$8500

#240
Tin String Holder
Circa 1930's
16" x 22"
$1000

#241
Cardboard with
Plastic Bottles
Circa 1960's
16" x 18" x 10"
$400

#242
Four Section Fold Out
Window Display
Circa 1950's
72" x 36"
$450

#243
Cardboard Box
Circa 1940's
8" x 10" x 12"
$1000

#244
Cardboard with Plastic Caps
Circa 1950's – 10" x 13" x 5"
$175

#245
Chalk Ware with Bottle
Circa 1940's
7" x 11" x 5"
$900

DISPLAYS

#246
Cardboard with
Mirror Back
Circa 1950's
15" x 36"
$400

#247
Cardboard with Wood Base
and Original Bottle
1938 – 16" x 24"
$650

#248
Cardboard Easel Back with Original Bottle
Circa 1920's
16" x 24"
$950 (Display only)

#249
Tin Bottle Rack
Circa 1930's
47" x 27"
$2200

DISPENSERS

#250
Milkglass Base
Circa 1930's
9" Diameter x 14" High
$2000

#251
Stainless Steel
Circa 1950's
12" x 24" x 18"
$400

#252
(Two Views)
Circa 1950's
12" x 18" x 12"
$300

#253
China
Circa 1900's
8" x 24"
$12,000

#254
Aluminum Tapper Keg
Circa 1960's – 5 Gal.
$100

#255
Tin and plastic
Circa 1950's – Four Gallon Jug
$350

DOOR PUSHES

#256
Tin (Canadian)
(Yellow)
Circa 1930's
4" x 12"
$750

#257
Reverse Glass
with Metal
Frame
Circa 1930's
4" x 12"
$600

#258
Tin (French-
Canadian)
Circa 1930's
4" x 13"
$500

#259
Tin/Bakelite Handle
Circa 1930's
3" x 12"
$600

#260
Porcelain (Canadian-French)
Circa 1940's
30" x 3"
$150

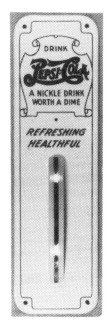

#261
Porcelain with
Bakelite Handle
Circa 1930's
3" x 12"
$950

#262
Tin
Circa 1940's
3" x 10"
$350

#263
Tin with Bakelite
Handle
Circa 1930's
3" x 12"
$750

FANS

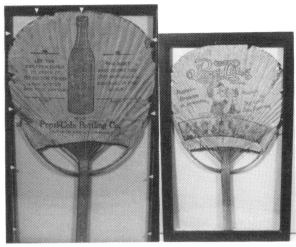

#264
Paper with Rattan Handle
(Two Views)
1905
10" x 12"
$1400

#265
Cardboard with
Wood Handle
Circa 1930's
8" x 12"
$300

#266
Cardboard with Wood Handle
(Mexican)
Circa 1940's
10" x 10"
$225

#267
Cardboard with Wicker Handle
Circa 1930's
8" x 10"
$225

#268
Cardboard with Wood
Handle – Circa 1940's
10" x 10"
$75

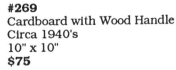

#269
Cardboard with Wood Handle
Circa 1940's
10" x 10"
$75

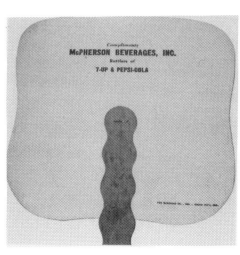

FOOD RELATED ITEMS

#270
China Bowl
Circa 1940's
4 3/4" Diameter
$225

#271
China Dessert Plate
Circa 1940's
7" Diameter
$225

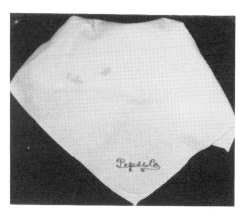

#272
Cloth Napkin
Circa 1940's
19" x 19"
$25

#273
Salt and Peppers
with Box (Decal Labels)
Circa 1930's
4"
$125

#274
Ice Cream Cup Lid
Circa 1940's
2" Diameter
$25

FOOD RELATED ITEMS

#275
Metal Ice Tongs
Circa 1950's
12"
$35

#277
Plastic Soda Spoons
(Five Different Colors)
Circa 1940's – 8"
$35 ea.

#276
Spoon with Enameled
Bottle Cap
Circa 1950's – 6"
$50

#279
Plastic Salt and Pepper Shaker
Circa 1950's
3" x 4"
$50

#278
Plastic Spoon Rest
Circa 1950's
5" x 6"
$25

#280
Popcorn Bucket
Circa 1950's
8" x 8"
$25

#281
Plastic Salt and
Pepper Shaker
Circa 1970's
3" x 4"
$20

#282
Paper Napkin
Circa 1940's
16" x 16"
$25

JEWELRY

#283
Metal Tie Bar
Circa 1970's
2"
$10

#284
Metal Tie Bar
Circa 1970's
2"
$10

#285
Metal Tie Bar
Circa 1970's
2"
$10

#286
Metal Tie Bar
Circa 1950's
2 1/2"
$50

#287
Metal Tie Bar
Circa 1970's
2"
$10

#288
Metal Tie Bar
Circa 1970's
3"
$10

#289
Bowling League Ring
1960's
$75

#290
Pocket Knife
(Pearl Handle)
Circa 1950's
1 1/2"
$85

#291
Celluloid/Tin
Stickpin
Circa 1950's
1" Diameter
$100

#292
Money Clip
Circa 1970's
1" x 2"
$25

#293
Money Clip
Circa 1950's
1" x 2"
$50

#294
Money Clip
Circa 1970's
1" x 2"
$25

#295
Pocket Knife/
Money Clip
Circa 1960's
2" x 1"
$20

#296
Pocket Knife
Circa 1950's
3 1/2"
$75

#297
Pocket Knife
Circa 1950's
3"
$25

#298
Metal Charm
with Key
Circa 1930's
1" Diameter
$75

#299
Compact
Circa 1950's
3" x 3"
$75

#300
Metal Charm
Circa 1930's
1" Diameter
$100

#301
Tie Bar with
Enamel Bottle Cap
Circa 1950's – 3"
$35

#302
Money Clip
Circa 1950's
2" Diameter
$50

#303
Ring (San Antonio, TX)
Circa 1970's
$75

#304
Ring (Los Angeles, CA)
Circa 1960's
$75

#305
Ring (Zanesville, OH)
Circa 1960's
$100

#306
Letterhead
(Richmond, VA)
1920
8 1/2" x 11"
$75

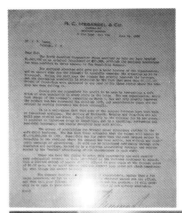

#307
Letter to Perspective
Stock Purchasers
for Pepsi Stock.
1922
8 1/2" x 11" with
Stock Order Form
$50

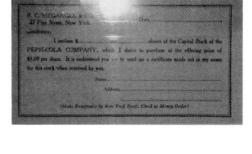

#308
Letterhead
(Greensboro, NC)
1916
8 1/2" x 11"
$100

#309
Check
1946
10" x 3"
$10

#310
Stock Certificate
1936
11" x 8 1/2"
$25

#311
Sale Bill for
C. Bradhams
Father's Estate
1894
8 1/2" x 11"
$50

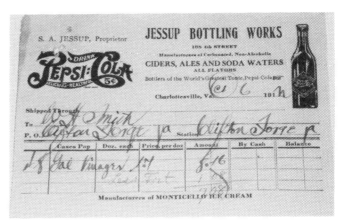

#312
Invoice
1913
7" x 4"
$35

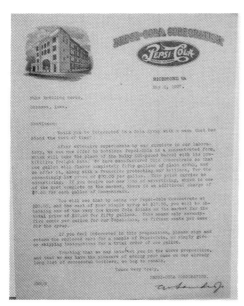

#313
Letterhead (Richmond, VA)
1927
8 1/2" x 11"
$75

#314
Letterhead and
Business Card
Circa 1930's
8 1/2" x 11"
$75

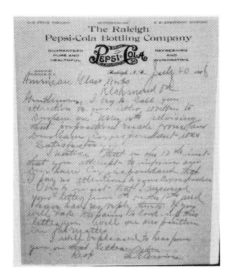

#315
Raleigh, NC Letterhead
1908
8 1/2" x 11"
$100

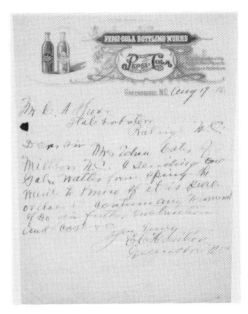

#316
Greensboro, NC
1916
8 1/2" x 11"
$100

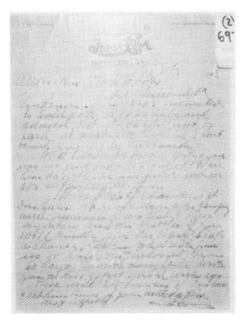

#317
Raleigh, NC Letterhead
1908
8 1/2" x 11"
$100

#318
Salesman's Contest Form
Circa 1940's
8 1/2" x 11"
$50

MAGAZINE AND NEWSPAPER ADS

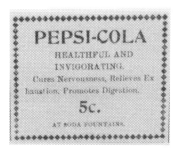

#319
Newspaper Ad
Circa 1910's
5" x 5"
$25

#320
Newspaper Ad
Circa 1910's
2" x 4"
$25

#321
Newspaper Ad
Circa 1910's
4" x 8"
$25

#322
Newspaper Ad
Circa 1910's – 3" x 4"
$45

#323
Magazine Ad
Circa 1940's – 11" x 14"
$25

#324
Newspaper Ad
Circa 1930's – 2" x 4"
$25

#325
Newspaper Ad
1913
5" x 5"
$25

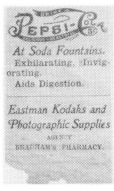

#326
Newspaper Ad
Circa 1900's
4" x 5"
$25

#327
Newspaper Ad
Circa 1910's
6" x 12"
$65

#328
Newspaper Ad
Circa 1930's
8" x 6"
$25

#329
Newspaper Ad
Circa 1900's
5" x 4"
$25

#330
Comic Page
Circa 1930's
4" x 20"
$60

#331
Newpaper Ad
Circa 1930's
4" x 14"
$25

#332
Newspaper Ad
Circa 1930's
4" x 14"
$25

#333
Comic Page
Circa 1930's
18" x 6"
$40

#334
Newspaper Ad
1908
4" x 20"
$60

#335
Comic Page
Circa 1930's
18" x 6"
$40

#336
Comic Page
Circa 1930's
18" x 6"
$40

#337
Newspaper Ad
Circa 1910's
8" x 6"
$45

#338
Newspaper Ad
Circa 1910's
8" x 8"
$60

#339
Newspaper Ad
Circa 1910's
8" x 8"
$45

#340
Newspaper Ad
Circa 1910's
4" x 8"
$45

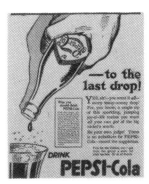

#341
Newspaper Ad
Circa 1910's
4" x 8"
$45

#342
Newspaper Ad
Circa 1910's
8" x 8"
$45

#343
Newspaper Ad
Circa 1910's
4' x 8"
$60

#344
Newspaper Ad
Circa 1910's
8" x 8"
$45

#345
Newspaper Ad
Circa 1910's
8" x 8"
$45

MAGAZINE AND NEWSPAPER ADS

#346
Newspaper Ad
Circa 1910's
8" x 8"
$60

#347
Newspaper Ad
Circa 1910's
4" x 8"
$45

#348
Newspaper Ad
Circa 1910's
6" x 10"
$45

#349
Newspaper Ad
Circa 1910's
6" x 10"
$45

#350
Newspaper Ad
Circa 1910's
8" x 12"
$45

#351
Newspaper Ad
1920
8" x 11"
$45

#352
Newspaper Ad
Circa 1910's
8" x 12"
$60

#353
Newspaper Ad
Circa 1910's
4" x 8"
$60

#354
Newspaper Ad
Circa 1910's
6" x 10"
$60

#355
Newspaper Ad
Circa 1930's
6" x 12"
$60

#356
Newspaper Ad
Circa 1930's
6" x 10"
$60

#357
Newspaper Ad
1962
Double Page
$85

#358
Newspaper Ad
Circa 1910's
6" x 8"
$45

#359
Newspaper Ad
Circa 1910's
8" x 11"
$45

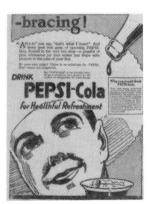

#360
Newspaper Ad
Circa 1910's
8" x 11"
$60

#361
Newspapaer Ad
Circa 1910's
8" x 11"
$45

#362
Newspaper Ad
Circa 1910's
8" x 11"
$60

MAGAZINE AND NEWSPAPER ADS

#363
Newspaper Ad
Circa 1910's
8" x 12"
$60

#364
Newspaper Ad
1909
8" x 12"
$60

#365
Newspaper Ad
Circa 1910's
8" x 11"
$60

#366
Newspaper Ad
1909
8" x 12"
$60

#367
Newspaper Ad
Circa 1910's
8" x 11"
$60

#368
Newspaper Ad
Circa 1910's
8" x 12"
$60

#369
Newspaper Ad
1909
8" x 11"
$60

#370
Newspaper Ad
Circa 1910's
8" x 12"
$60

#371
Newspapaer Ad
Circa 1910's
8" x 11"
$60

#372
Newspaper Ad
Circa 1910's
8" x 11"
$60

#373
Newspaper Ad
Circa 1910's
8" x 12"
$60

#374
Newspaper Ad
Circa 1910's
8" x 11"
$60

#375
Newspaper Ad
Circa 1910's
8" x 11"
$60

#376
Newspaper Ad
Circa 1910's
10" x 12"
$60

#377
Newspaper Ad
Circa 1910's
8" x 11"
$60

#378
Newspaper Ad
Circa 1910's
8" x 10"
$45

#379
Newspaper Ad
Circa 1910's
8" x 10"
$45

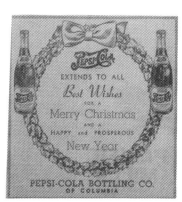

#380
Newspapaer Ad
Circa 1930's
10" x 10"
$25

MENUS

#381
Two Sheet
Circa 1960's
16" x 11"
$25

#382
Two Sheet (Two Views)
Circa 1940's
16" x 11"
$100

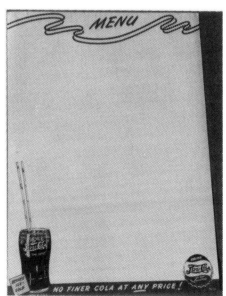

#383
One Sheet
Circa 1940's
8" x 11"
$50

#384
One Sheet
Circa 1940's
8" x 11"
$25

PAMPHLETS AND BOOKLETS

#385
Merchandising
Equipment Binder
Circa 1950's
6" x 10"
$75

#386
Notepad
1920
2" x 4"
$100

#387
Notepad
Circa 1930's
3" x 7"
$50

#388
Bottlers Program
1958
8 1/2" x 11"
$35

#389
Sales Program
1954
8 1/2" x 11"
$35

#390
Dispenser
Maintenance Manual
Circa 1940's
6" x 10"
$50

#391
Pepsi World
Magazine
1959 – 8 1/2" x 11"
$10

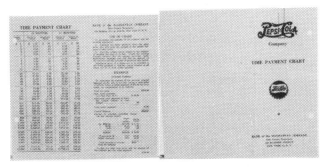

#392
Payment Chart – (Two Views)
Circa 1940's
11" x 11"
$50

#393
Coronation Program
Circa 1950's
3" x 5"
$75

#394
Convention Program
1954
8 1/2" x 11"
$35

#395
Convention Program
1947
6" x 12"
$75

#396
Routeman's Info. Sheet
Circa 1950's
5" x 3"
$10

#397
Convention Program
1954
8 1/2" x 11"
$25

#398
School Booklet
Circa 1940's
12" x 8"
$75

PAMPHLETS AND BOOKLETS

#399
Pepsi World Magazine
1956
8 1/2" x 11"
$25

#400
Pepsi World Magazine
Circa 1950's
8 1/2" x 11"
$10

#401
Bottle Profit Table
Circa 1960's
4" x 6"
$50

#402
Story of Pepsi Cola
Circa 1950's
12" x 6"
$25

#403
Fountain Syrup
Profit Table
Circa 1950's
3" x 7"
$50

#404
Baseball Record Book
1952
4" x 8"
$25

#405
Pepsi World Magazine
1964
8 1/2" x 11"
$10

#406
Advertising Book
Circa 1940's
12" x 16"
$75

#407
Beverage Book
Circa 1970's
6" x 12"
$10

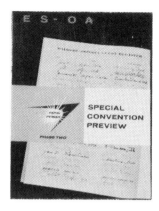

#408
Pepsi World Magazine
1960
8 1/2" x 11"
$10

#409
Vinyl Notebook with
Merchandising of
Equipment
Circa 1950's
5" x 8"
$150

#410
Miss America Program
and Letter
1958
8 1/2" x 11"
$50

#411
Choice-Vend Coolers
(Two Views)
Circa 1960's
6" x 12"
$100

#412
Fold-Out
Circa 1940's
8 1/2" x 12"
$75

#413
Football Program
Circa 1960's – 17" x 11"
$25

#414
Football Program
Circa 1960's – 17" x 11"
$25

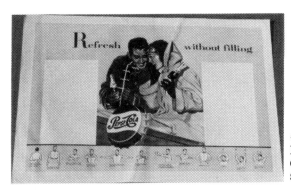

#415
Football Program
Circa 1950's – 17" x 11"
$35

#416
Pepsi World Newspaper
1954
24" x 30"
$25

#417
Baseball Scorecard
(Richmond, VA)
1919
12" x 16"
$150

PATCHES

#418
Cloth
Circa 1960's
2" x 2"
$10

#419
Cloth
Circa 1960's
3" x 2"
$15

#420
Cloth (NHRA)
Circa 1970's
3" Diameter
$10

#421
Cloth
Circa 1960's
3" x 1"
$10

#422
Cloth (NASCAR)
Circa 1970's
4" x 2"
$10

#423
Uniform Patch
Circa 1960's
9" x 6"
$20

#424
Cloth (NASCAR)
Circa 1970's
4" x 2"
$10

PENS AND PENCILS

#425
Mechanical Pencil (Martin, TN)
Circa 1940's – 6"   **$100**

#426
Mechanical Pencil
(with Floating Bottle)
Circa 1940's – 5"
$175

#427
Plastic Pen
Circa 1960's – 5"
$15

#428
Mechanical Pencil
1950's – 6"
$60

#429
Bottle Cap on End
(Mechanical Pencil)
Circa 1960's – 5"
$35

#430
Marking Pen
Circa 1950's – 5"
$40

#431
Mechanical Pencil (Card-board)
Circa 1940's – 6"
$85

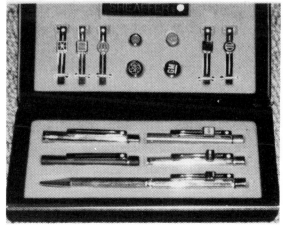

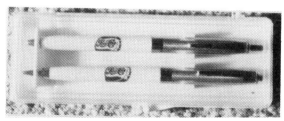

#432
Ball Point Pen and
Mechanical Pencil with Box
Circa 1950's
5"
$60 Set

#433
Sheaffer Set (Two are Pepsi)
Circa 1970's
8" x 4"
$50

PENS AND PENCILS

#434
Wooden Pencil
Circa 1940's – 9"   **$35**

#435
Celluloid Bullet Pencil
Circa 1950's – 5"
$50

#436
Mechanical Pencil (Petersburg, W.VA)
Circa 1940's – 6"
$125

#437
Mechanical Pencil (Quincy, IL)
Circa 1950's – 6"
$60

#438
Mechanical Pencil
Circa 1940's – 7"
$125

#439
Ball Point Pen
Circa 1950's – 7"
$60

#440
Mechanical Pencil
Circa 1940's – 6"
$125

#441
Bullet Pencil (Celluloid)
Circa 1910's – 3"
$200

PHOTOGRAPHS

#442
Joan Crawford
Circa 1970's – 8" x 10"
$25

#443
Joan Crawford
Circa 1970's – 8" x 10"
$25

#444
Miss Virginia (Autographed)
Circa 1950's
8" x 10"
$25

#445
B & W
Circa 1930's
10" x 14"
$100

#446
Billboard
Circa 1970's – 8 1/2" x 11"
$10

#447
Copy Negative of
Seth Thomas Clock
Circa 1930's – 8" x 5"
$50

PHOTOGRAPHS

#448
Soda Fountain with Pepsi Sign
Circa 1910 – 10" x 8"
$125

#449
Delivery Wagon
Circa 1900's – 8" x 10"
$100

#450
First Pepsi Truck
Circa 1900's
8 1/2" x 6"
$100

#451
New Bern N.C. Home Office
Circa 1900's
11" x 8"
$100

#452
Caleb Bradham
Circa 1900's
5" x 7 1/2"
$100

PINBACKS

#453
Celluloid/Tin
Circa 1960's
3"
$50

#454
Celluloid/Tin
Circa 1970's
1"
$25

#455
Celluloid/Tin
Circa 1970's
2"
$10

#456
Celluloid/Tin
Circa 1970's
3"
$10

#457
Seattle Pilots Baseball
1969
2"x 1"
$25

#458
Celluloid/Tin
Circa 1940's
1"
$50

#459
Celluloid/Tin
Circa 1950's
4"
$50

#460
Celluloid/Tin
Circa 1970's
2"
$25

#461
Celluloid/Tin
Circa 1970's
2"
$10

#462
Celluloid/Tin
Circa 1960's
4"
$10

#463
Celluloid/Tin
Circa 1970's
2"
$10

#464
Celluloid/Tin
Circa 1970's
4"
$10

#465
Tin
Circa 1970's
2"
$10

#466
Celluloid/Tin
Circa 1970's
3"
$25

#467
Celluloid/Tin
Circa 1970's
2"
$10

#468
Celluloid/Tin
Circa 1970's
2"
$10

#469
Plastic
Circa 1970's
4" x 4"
$25

#470
Celluloid/Tin
Circa 1970's
3"
$10

PINBACKS

#471
Celluloid/Tin
Circa 1960's
1"
$10

#472
Arabic
Celluloid/Tin
Circa 1950's
1"
$25

#473
Celluloid/Tin
Circa 1940's
1"
$75

#474
Celluloid/Tin
Circa 1950's
2"
$25

#475
Madison, IN Regatta
1967
3" x 2"
$10

#476
Celluloid/Tin
Circa 1970's
2"
$25

#477
Celluloid/Tin
Circa 1970's
4"
$10

#478
Celluloid/Tin
Circa 1970's
2"
$10

#479
Celluloid/Tin
Circa 1970's
2"
$10

#480
Celluloid/Tin
Circa 1970's
2"
$10

#481
Celluloid/Tin
with Ribbon
Circa 1950's
2"
$75

#482
Celluloid/Tin
with Ribbon
Circa 1950's
2"
$50

#483
Celluloid/Tin
with Ribbon
Circa 1950's
2"
$50

#484
Celluloid/Tin
Circa 1960's
2"
$50

#485
Celluloid/Tin
Circa 1950's
2"
$25

#486
Celluloid/Tin
Circa 1970's
2"
$10

#487
Celluloid/Tin
Circa 1950's
3"
$50

#488
Celluloid/Tin
Circa 1950's
3"
$50

#489
Celluloid/Tin
Circa 1950's
2"
$50

PLAYING CARDS

#490
Quincy, IL
(Original Box – Yellow)
Circa 1940's
3" x 4"
$125

#491
Long Island City, NY
(Original Box)
Circa 1940's
3" x 4"
$150

#492
Original Box
Circa 1940's
3" x 4"
$175

#493
Quincy, IL
(Original Box – Maroon)
Circa 1940's
3" x 4"
$125

#494
Quincy, IL
(Original Box – Blue)
Circa 1940's
3" x 4"
$125

#495
Cedar Rapids, IA
Circa 1950's
4" x 3"
$150

#496
N.Y. Worlds Fair
1964
4" x 3"
$65

#497
Memphis, MO
(Rockwell Art)
Circa 1970's
3" x 4"
$35

#498
Mountain Dew
Circa 1970's
3" x 4"
$25

RULERS

#499
Plastic
Circa 1960's – 12"
$15

#500
Tin
Circa 1950's
12"
$20

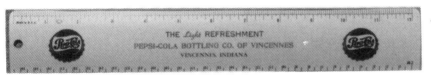

#501
Tin
Circa 1950's
12"
$20

#502
Tin
Circa 1950's
12"
$20

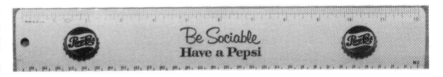

#503
Plastic
Circa 1950's
12"
$15

RULERS

#504
Wooden (Lexington, VA)
Circa 1940's
12"
$75

#505
Wooden
Circa 1940's
12"
$75

#506
Tin
Circa 1950's
12"
$20

#507
Tin
Circa 1950's
12"
$35

#508
Tin
Circa 1950's
12"
$20

CARDBOARD SIGNS

#509
Die Cut Easel
Back
Circa 1930's
10" x 14"
$850

#510
Two Sided Die Cut
Circa 1930's
12" x 12"
$325

#511
Die Cut Easel Back
Circa 1930's
7" x 8"
$650

#512
Two Sided Die Cut
Circa 1930's
14" x 14"
$325

#513
Two Sided Die Cut
Circa 1930's
14" x 14"
$325

#514
Two Sided Die Cut
Circa 1930's
14" x 14"
$325

CARDBOARD SIGNS

#515
Die Cut Bottle Topper
Circa 1940's – 5" x 10"
$650

#516
Die Cut Easel Back
Circa 1930's
8" x 12"
$750

#517
Trolley Sign – Yellow Background
Circa 1930's – 21" x 11"
$1600

#519
Trolley Sign – Yellow Background
Circa 1940's – 21" x 11"
$1800

#518
Easel Back
Circa 1930's – 12" x 30"
$900

CARDBOARD SIGNS

#520
Trolley Sign
Circa 1940's
28" x 11"
$350

#521
Trolley Sign
Circa 1940's
28" x 11"
$425

#522
Trolley Sign
Circa 1950's
28" x 11"
$125

#523
Original Frame
Circa 1940's
28" x 11"
$500

#524
Trolley Sign
Circa 1940's
28" x 11"
$375

#525
Trolley Sign
Circa 1940's
28" x 11"
$375

CARDBOARD SIGNS

#526
Back Bar Festoon
Circa 1940's
$2500

#527
Trolley Sign in Original Frame
Circa 1940's
28" x 11"
$450

#528
Trolley Sign
Circa 1950's
28" x 11"
$125

#529
Trolley Sign
Circa 1950's
28" x 11"
$125

#530
Trolley Sign
Circa 1950's
28" x 11"
$125

CARDBOARD SIGNS

#531
Self Framed
Circa 1930's
25" x 34"
$1000

#532
Easel Back
Circa 1930's
18" x 26"
$1200

#533
Self Framed
Circa 1930's
25" x 34"
$1000

#534
Self Framed
Circa 1930's
25" x 34"
$900

#535
Self Framed
Circa 1930's
25" x 34"
$900

#536
Poster
Circa 1940's
26" x 33"
$450

#537
Embossed
(Hamilton King Art)
1909 – 9" x 9"
$2500

#538
Embossed
(Hamilton King Artwork)
1909 – 9" x 9"
$2500

#539
Self Framed
Circa 1930's
25' x 34"
$1200

#540
Poster
Circa 1960's – 38" x 28"
$50

#541
Die Cut Bottle Topper
Circa 1950's
7" x 12"
$50

#542
Trolley Sign
Circa 1960's – 28" x 11"
$35

#543
Easel Back
Circa 1940's
18" x 26"
$650

#544
Easel-Back
Circa 1940's
18" x 27"
$650

Item #758

Item #708

Item #667

Item #734

Item #666

Item #648

Item #670

Item #533

Item #645

Item #634

Item #120

Item #622

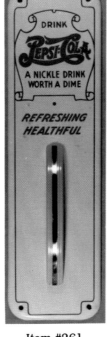

Item #261

Item #723

Item #151

Item #732

Item #519

Item #115

Item #509

Item #552

Item #546

Item #759

Item #163

Item #668

Item #671

Item #752

Item #579

Item #517

Item #539

Item #535

Item #564

Item #531

Item #534

Item #114

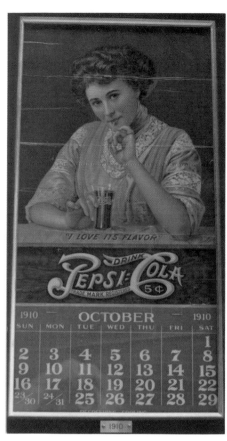

Item #118

Item #554

Item #121

Item #253

Item #245

Item #727

Item #613

CARDBOARD SIGNS

#545
Die Cut Easel Back
Circa 1950's
50"
$250

#546
Easel Back
Circa 1940's
14"
$375

#547
Foil Covered
Circa 1940's
5" x 18"
$225

#548
Die Cut Easel Back
Circa 1930's
5" x 18"
$550

#549
Die Cut Easel Back
Circa 1970's
18"
$50

#550
Die Cut Easel Back
Circa 1950's
48"
$300

#551
Fold Out Die Cut
Circa 1930's
20" x 16"
$850

CARDBOARD SIGNS

#552
Die Cut (Two Sided)
Circa 1930's
21" x 14"
$850

#553
Seven Piece Festoon
Circa 1930's
$2800

#554
Die Cut, 3-D
Easel Back
Circa 1930's
28 1/2" x 40"
$4000

#555
Die Cut Easel Back
Circa 1930's
8 1/2" x 12"
$1200

#556
Easel Back
Circa 1950's
14" x 14"
$100

#557
Easel Back
Circa 1950's
14" x 16"
$85

#558
Savannah Brewing Co.
Circa 1910
18" x 14"
$2200

#559
Savannah Brewing Co.
Circa 1910
18" x 14"
$2200

#560
Window Sign
Circa 1970's
24" x 30"
$25

#561
Easel Back
Circa 1950's
18" x 20"
$100

CARDBOARD SIGNS

#562
Poster – 1907
15 3/4" x 24"
$11,000

#563
Heavy Cardboard
1907 – 9" x 11"
$6000

#564
Poster
1909
20" x 25"
$5000

#565
Miss Pepsi Cola
(Original Frame)
1905 – 21" x 27"
$8500

CARDBOARD SIGNS

#566
Poster with Original Frame
Circa 1960's
38" x 28"
$65

#567
Die Cut Easel Back
Circa 1940's
70"
$1100

#568
Poster with Original Frame
Circa 1950's
38" x 28"
$150

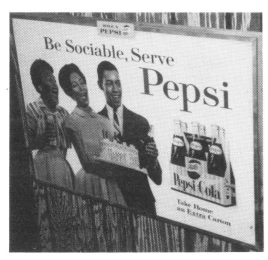

#569
Poster with Original Frame
Circa 1950's
28" x 18"
$175

#570
Poster
Circa 1970's
18" x 30"
$25

CARDBOARD SIGNS

#571
Easel Back
Circa 1910's
20" x 30"
$5000

#572
Easel Back
Circa 1910's
18" x 24"
$5000

#573
Trolley Sign – Petty Art
(Could Be New)
Circa 1940's
28" x 11"
Reference Only

#574
Original Wood Frame
Circa 1940's
28" x 21"
$800

#575
Easel Back
Circa 1950's
11 1/2" x 14"
$100

#576
Easel Back
Circa 1950's
24" x 24"
$50

#577
Die Cut Easel Back
Circa 1950's
34" x 48"
$350

#578
Poster
Circa 1960's
38" x 28"
$35

#579
Hanger
Circa 1940's
20" Diameter
$500

#580
Die Cut Bottle Topper
Circa 1950's
5" x 10"
$250

CARDBOARD SIGNS

#581
Trolley Sign with Original Frame
Yellow Background
Circa 1950's
28" x 11"
$200

#582
Trolley Sign with Original Frame
Yellow Background
Circa 1950's
28" x 11"
$200

#583
Trolley
Circa 1950's
28" x 11"
$125

#584
Trolley
Circa 1950's
28" x 11"
$125

#585
Poster with Original Frame
Circa 1950's
38" x 28"
$200

#586
Trolley Sign (Canadian)
Circa 1940's
22" x 12"
$500

CARDBOARD SIGNS

#587
Trolley Sign
Circa 1950's
28" x 11"
$125

#588
Trolley
Circa 1950's
28" x 11"
$125

#589
Easel Back (3-D)
Circa 1950's
16" x 22"
$85

#590
Trolley Sign
Circa 1950's
28" x 11"
$125

#591
Poster with Original Frame
Yellow Background
Circa 1950's
38" x 28"
$200

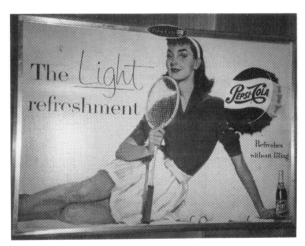

#592
Poster with Original Frame
Yellow Background
Circa 1950's
38" x 28"
$200

CARDBOARD SIGNS

#593
Easel Back
Circa 1930's
40" x 22"
$450

#594
Foil Covered
Circa 1960's
8" x 8"
$25

#595
Channel Sign
Circa 1950's
22" x 7"
$50

#596
Channel Sign
Circa 1950's
22" x 7"
$50

#597
Open/Closed (Two Views)
Circa 1950's
12" x 12"
$125

CARDBOARD SIGNS

#598
Sepia Tones
Circa 1930's
16" x 11"
$350

#599
Hanger
Circa 1930's
8" x 16"
$550

#600
Light Cardboard
Circa 1940's
56" x 32"
$150

#601
Foil Covered
Circa 1960's
14" x 6"
$25

#602
Easel Back
Circa 1950's
14" x 11"
$75

#603
Foil Covered
Circa 1960's
14" x 11"
$25

#604
Window Sign
Circa 1930's
11" x 14"
$75

#605
Grocery Orderer
Circa 1930's
8" x 14"
$50

#606
Carton Stuffer
Circa 1950's
12" Diameter
$25

#607
Heavy Cardboard
Circa 1950's
40" x 16"
$100

#608
Foil Covered
Circa 1960's – 16" x 24"
$50

#609
Window Sign
Circa 1950's – 14" x 22"
$75

CARDBOARD SIGNS

#610
From Bottlers Convention
Circa 1970's
14" x 18"
$15

#611
From Bottlers
Convention
Circa 1970's
14" x 18"
$15

#612
Standup
1962
8" x 6"
$100

#613
Die Cut 3-D
1917
20" x 34"
$8500

#614
Foil Covered
Circa 1960's
13" x 12"
$100

#615
Headquarters Building
(Original Artwork)
1938
34" x 25"
$800

#616
Trolley Sign
Circa 1940's
28" x 11"
$325

#617
Foil Covered
Circa 1960's
12" x 8"
$25

#618
Hanger
Circa 1940's
30" x 16"
$350

CELLULOID SIGNS

#619
Celluloid Over Tin
Circa 1940's
4" Diameter
$450

#620
Celluloid/Tin
Circa 1940's
9" Diameter
$2500

#621
Celluloid/Tin
Circa 1930's
9" Diameter
$375

#622
Celluloid/Tin
Circa 1930's
5" x 13"
$850

#623
Celluloid/Tin
Circa 1940's
9" Diameter
$250

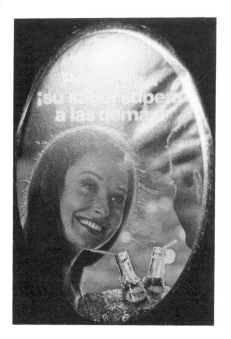

#624
Celluloid/Tin
Circa 1960's
8" x 12"
$85

#625
Celluloid/Tin
Circa 1940's
9" Diameter
$300

#626
Celluloid/Tin
Circa 1940's
9" Diameter
$375

GLASS SIGNS

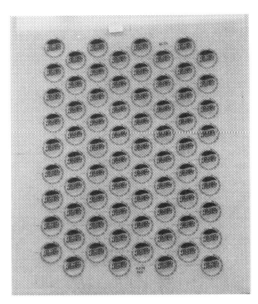

#627
Glass Printing Plate
Circa 1950's
14" x 17"
$100

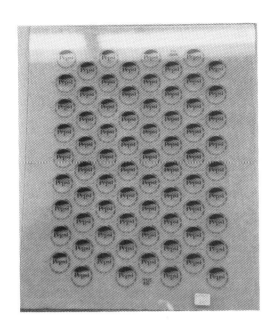

#628
Glass Printing Plate
Circa 1950's
14" x 17"
$100

#629
Glass Negative
Circa 1960's
12" x 16"
$75

#630
Glass Negative
Circa 1960's
12" x 16"
$75

#631
Reverse Glass
Circa 1940's
4" x 12"
$400

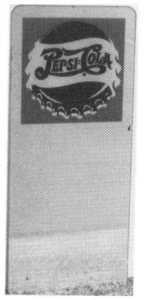

#632
Reverse Glass
Circa 1940's
6" x 13"
$400

#633
Mirror with Wood Frame
Circa 1930's
14" x 10"
$1600

#634
Reverse Glass with
Foil Backing
Circa 1930's
12" x 10"
$1800

LIGHT-UP SIGNS

#635
Plastic
Circa 1950's
12" x 8"
$200

#636
Plastic Revolving
Circa 1950's
30" x 18"
$300

#637
Plastic Revolving
Circa 1960's
17" x 17"
$300

#638
Plastic with
Metal Frame
(Yellow Background)
Circa 1950's
10" x 18"
$150

#639
Embossed Plastic and
Metal Frame
(Revolving Cylinders)
Circa 1960's – 30" x 30"
$550

#640
Plastic and Metal
Circa 1950's
16" x 16"
$200

#641
Metal Frame Plastic Front
Circa 1950's
19" x 9"
$500

#642
Plastic Revolving
Circa 1950's
30" x 18"
$475

#643
Plastic
Circa 1950's
10" Diameter
$250

#644
Plastic and Metal
Circa 1960's
16" x 8"
$100

#645
Chalkware and
Reverse Glass 3-D
Circa 1930's
12" x 17"
$8500

#646
Plastic with Metal Frame
(Revolving) – (Two Views)
Circa 1950's – 16" x 12"
$400

#647
Revolving
Circa 1960's
10" x 14"
$35

LIGHT-UP SIGNS

#648
Plastic Front Metal Frame
Revolving Cylinder
Circa 1950's
20 1/2" x 10" x 7 1/2"
$750

#649
Patio Lights/Box
Circa 1970's
12" x 4" x 5"
$25

#650
Plastic
Circa 1940's
10" x 14"
$600

#651
Neon
Circa 1940's
15" x 6"
$1500

#652
Neon
Circa 1970's
30" x 15"
$600

#653
Plastic
Circa 1950's
15" Diameter
$400

#654
Neon with Metal and
Wood Frame
Circa 1930's
14" x 8"
$3000

#655
Glass with Metal Frame
Circa 1940's
16" Diameter
$850

#656
Plastic Front
Circa 1940's
19" x 9"
$950

#657
Corkboard with
Metal Frame
Circa 1970's
30" x 20"
$25

#658
Window Decal
Circa 1960's
6" x 6"
$50

#659
Wooden Truck Sign
Circa 1960's
66" x 12"
$300

#660
Tin Menu Board
Circa 1960's
30" x 24"
$50

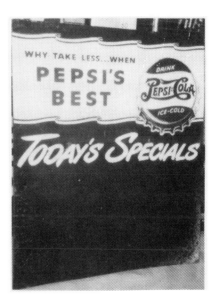

#661
Tin Menu Board
Circa 1940's
20" x 27"
$350

#662
Window Decal
Circa 1960's
11" x 14"
$75

#663
Cardboard with
Tin Frame
Menu Board
Circa 1940's
13" x 21"
$375

#664
Window Decal
Circa 1950's
8" x 12"
$50

#665
3-D Masonite
Circa 1950's
12" x 12"
$175

#666
Wooden Menu Board
Circa 1940's
14" x 32"
$675

#667
Paper (Pictures Foil
Covered Bottle)
1934
16" x 12"
$1300

#668
Heavy Paper
Circa 1940's
24" x 36"
$900

#669
Paper Banner
1940
42" x 76"
$2000

#670
Poster
Circa 1940's
36" x 24"
$600

#671
Window Decal
Circa 1940's
12" x 18"
$600

#673
Double Sided
Fold Over
Circa 1940's
24" x 18"
$75

#672
Hanging Lamp Shade
Circa 1970's
16" Diameter
$35

#674
Broadside
Circa 1940's
16" x 24"
$100

#675
Broadside
Circa 1930's
14" x 18"
$375

#676
Broadside
Circa 1940's
14" x 20"
$150

#677
Broadside
Circa 1940's
14" x 20"
$150

#678
Banner
Circa 1950's
16" x 24"
$25

#679
Newspaper Broadside
Circa 1950's
14" x 20"
$75

PAPER SIGNS

#680
Corregated
Circa 1950's
28" x 12"
$25

#681
Window Sign
Circa 1970's
25" x 11"
$25

#682
Banner
Circa 1950's
18" x 6"
$50

#683
Window Sign
Circa 1940's
24" x 8"
$50

#684
Window Decal
Circa 1940's
8" x 5"
$125

PAPER SIGNS

#685
Banner
Circa 1950's
8" x 16"
$25

#686
Window Decal
Circa 1970's
14" x 12"
$25

#687
Window Decal
Circa 1970's
14" x 12"
$25

#688
Window Decal
Circa 1960's
14" x 12"
$25

#689
Window Sign
Circa 1950's
22" x 7"
$25

#690
Window Stick-On
Circa 1950's
19" x 8"
$25

#691
Carton Sign
Circa 1950's
11" x 14"
$25

#692
Window Stick-On
Circa 1950's
19" x 8"
$25

PLASTIC SIGNS

#693
Three Dimensional
Circa 1960's
11" x 14"
$50

#694
Metal Frame
(Machine Sign)
Circa 1950's
12" Diameter
$75

#695
Metal Framed
Circa 1960's
16" x 6"
$50

#696
3-D/Masonite
20" x 10"
$350

#697
Window Sign
Circa 1950's
10" x 8"
$75

#698
Machine Sign
Circa 1950's
28" x 11"
$225

#699
Moulded
Circa 1960's
10" x 10"
$50

#700
Wood Frame
Circa 1950's
72" x 18"
$150

#701
Original Frame
Circa 1960's
18" x 16"
$200

#702
Golf Tournament
Sponsorship Sign
Circa 1970's
30" x 15"
$25

#703
Salesman Sample
(New) 5" x 8"
Reference Only

#704
Rack Sign
Circa 1950's
18" x 18"
$250

#705
Canadian
Circa 1950's
26" x 11"
$300

#706
Rack Sign
Circa 1950's
18" x 18"
$250

#707
Single Sided (Canadian)
Circa 1950's
20" x 30"
$450

#708
Single Sided
Circa 1940's
18" x 44"
$1200

#709
Single Sided
Circa 1940's
30" x 10"
$1100

#710
Single Sided
Circa 1940's
16" x 12"
$1100

#711
Single Sided
Circa 1950's
48" x 30"
$300

TIN SIGNS

#712
Embossed
Circa 1960's
31" x 12"
$75

#713
Self Framed
Circa 1960's
6' x 3'
$275

#714
Self Framed
Circa 1960's
31" x 12"
$200

#715
Self Framed
Circa 1960's
28" x 40"
$150

#716
Tin/Cardboard
Circa 1960's
12" x 8"
$50

TIN SIGNS

#717
Shelf Strip
Circa 1940's
8"
$100

#718
Rack Sign
Circa 1960's
16" x 14"
$50

#719
Cooler Sign
Circa 1930's
28" x 11"
$150

#720
Rack Sign
Circa 1960's
14" x 14"
$50

#721
Embossed
Circa 1930's
18" x 54"
$1100

#722
Die Cut
Circa 1930's
12" x 45"
$650

#723
Embossed
1931
13" x 39"
$2000

#724
Embossed
Circa 1910's
26" x 6"
$1000

#725
Embossed
Circa 1910's
30" x 10"
$1000

#726
Embossed
Circa 1910's
30" x 20"
$1000

#727
Self Framed
1908 – 8 1/2" x 10 1/2"
$8500

TIN SIGNS

#728
Canadian Embossed
Circa 1930's
36" x 24"
$700

#729
Dispenser Sign
Circa 1940's
6" x 6"
$225

#730
Embossed
Circa 1930's
23" x 11 1/2"
$850

#731
Multi-Colored
Circa 1950's
20" x 28"
$350

#732
Thin Hammered
Tin
Circa 1930's
20" x 20"
$750

TIN SIGNS

#733
Embossed
Circa 1940's
50" x 36"
$475

#734
Window Corner Sign
Circa 1940's
12" x 12"
$375

#735
License Topper
Circa 1940's
12" x 7"
$375

#736
Self Framed
Circa 1950's
48" x 24"
$250

#737
Eight Piece Display Sign
Circa 1930's
8' x 5'
$2200

#738
Self Framed
Circa 1940's
48" x 24"
$450

TIN SIGNS

#739
Self Framed
Circa 1950's
24" x 28"
$75

#740
Self Framed
Circa 1950's
28" x 11"
$125

#741
Cash Register Topper
Circa 1940's
12" x 5"
$500

#742
Rack Sign
Circa 1950's
8" x 8"
$75

#743
Rack Sign
Circa 1950's
16" x 16"
$75

#744
Self Framed
Circa 1940's
48" x 30"
$425

TIN SIGNS

#745
Canadian
Circa 1940's
28" x 11"
$200

#746
Rack Sign
Circa 1960's
8" x 18"
$50

#747
Tin/Cardboard
Circa 1960's
5" x 5"
$25

#748
Embossed
Circa 1960's – 28" x 11"
$75

#749
Self Framed
Circa 1950's
14" x 42"
$150

#750
Rack Sign
Circa 1960's – 14" X 3"
$50

#751
Circa 1910 – 12" x 3"
$550

#752
Embossed
Circa 1910's
8" x 3"
$450

#753
Tin/Cardboard
Circa 1910
12" x 5"
$600

#754
3-D
Circa 1940's
31" Diameter
$750

#755
Embossed
Circa 1930's
21" x 4"
$650

#756
Two Sided Hanger
Circa 1940's
16" x 12"
$275

#757
Embossed (Red Background)
Circa 1910's
27 1/2" x 13 1/2"
$750

#758
Embossed (Canadian)
Circa 1940's
28" x 18"
$300

#759
Rack Sign
Circa 1950's
18" x 6"
$100

#760
Metal Lighter
Circa 1950's
2" x 1"
$25

#761
Metal Lighter
Circa 1940's
2"
$75

#762
Lighter with Original Bag
Circa 1950's
2" Diameter
$75

#763
Desk Lighter (Lucite)
Circa 1940's
5" x 5"
$50

#764
Metal Lighter
Circa 1950's
1" x 4"
$150

#765
Metal Lighter
Circa 1950's
2 1/4" x 1 1/2"
$75

#766
Can Lighter
Circa 1940's
12 oz. Can
$425

#767
Metal Lighter with
Enamel Insert
Circa 1940's
1 1/2" x 2 1/2"
$100

#768
Metal Lighter
Circa 1950's
1 1/2" x 3"
$50

SMOKING PARAPHERNALIA

#769
Metal Lighter
Circa 1950's
2 1/2" x 1 1/2"
$50

#770
Metal Lighter
Circa 1950's
2 1/2" x 1 1/2"
$25

#771
Metal Lighter
Circa 1970's
2" x 2"
$25

#772
Metal Lighter
Circa 1950's
2 1/2" x 1 1/2"
$75

#773
Metal Lighter
Circa 1950's
2 1/2" x 1 1/2"
$35

#774
Metal Lighter
Circa 1970's
2" x 2"
$25

#775
Metal Lighter
Circa 1950's
2 1/2" x 1 1/2"
$25

#776
Metal Lighter with
Enamel Insert
Circa 1960's
1 1/2" x 2 1/2"
$25

#777
Musical Lighter
(Two Views)
Circa 1950's
2" x 2"
$275

#778
Musical Lighter
(Two Views)
Circa 1950's
1 1/2" x 2 1/2"
$350

#779
Musical Lighter (Two Views)
Circa 1950's
2" x 3"
$350

#780
Musical Lighter/Box
(Three Views)
Circa 1950's
2" x 3"
$350

SMOKING PARAPHERNALIA

#781
Metal and
Plastic Lighter
Circa 1970's
1" x 3"
$25

#782
Metal and
Plastic Lighter
Circa 1950's
1 1/2" x 2 1/2"
$35

#783
Plastic Lighter
Circa 1960's
1 1/2" x 2 1/2"
$25

#784
Metal Lighter
Circa 1960's
1 1/2" x 2 1/2"
$25

#785
Metal Lighter
Circa 1960's
1 1/2" x 2"
$25

#786
Metal Lighter
Circa 1960's
2" x 3"
$25

#787
Metal Lighter
(Pensacola, FL)
Circa 1960's
1 1/2" x 2 1/2"
$25

#788
Metal Lighter
Circa 1970's
1 1/2" x 2 1/2"
$25

#789
Metal Lighter
Circa 1960's
1 1/2" x 2 1/2"
$25

#790
Metal Lighter
with Enamel Insert
Circa 1960's
1 1/2" x 2 1/2"
$25

#791
Metal Lighter with
Enamel Insert
Circa 1950's
1 1/2" x 2 1/2"
$75

SMOKING PARAPHERNALIA

#792
Matchbook
Circa 1940's
$30

#793
Matchbook
Circa 1950's
$15

#794
Matchbook
Circa 1940's
$30

#795
Matchbook
Circa 1940's
$20

#796
Matchbook
Circa 1930's
3" x 4"
$50

#797
Matchbook
Circa 1950
$25

#798
Matchbook
Circa 1940's
$25

#799
Matchbook
Circa 1930's
$40

#800
Matchbook
Circa 1940's
$30

#801
Matchbook
Circa 1950's
$20

#802
Matchbook
Circa 1940's
$30

SMOKING PARAPHERNALIA

#803
Glass Ashtray
Circa 1970's
4" x 4"
$25

#804
Cigarette Pack
Circa 1970's
2 1/2" x 3 1/2"
$10

#805
Glass Ashtray
Circa 1940's
4" Diameter
$85

#806
Glass Ashtray
Circa 1960's
4" x 4"
$25

#807
Tin Ashtray (Mexican)
Circa 1950's
4" Diameter
$25

#808
Glass Ashtray
(Memphis, MO)
Circa 1950's
4" x 4"
$60

#809
Glass Ashtray
Circa 1960's
4" x 4"
$35

#810
Glass Ashtray
(San Diego, CA)
1963
4" x 4"
$35

SMOKING PARAPHERNALIA

#811
Bakelite Ashtray
Circa 1950's
5" Diameter
$35

#812
Metal Ashtray with
Plastic Bottle Lighter
Circa 1950's
6" Diameter
$100

#813
Tin Ashtray with
Enameled Bottle Cap
Circa 1950's
4" Diameter
$100

#814
Bakelite Ashtray
(Yuba City, CA)
Circa 1950's
6" Diameter
$65

#815
Glass Ashtray
Circa 1950's
6" x 6"
$100

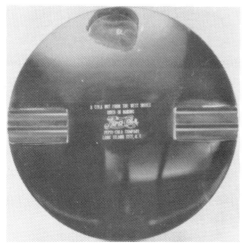

#816
Metal Ashtray
Circa 1950's – 8" Diameter
$65

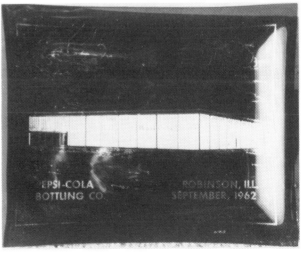

#817
Glass Ashtray (Robinson, IL)
1962 – 10" x 6"
$100

#818
Plastic Ashtray
Circa 1960's
5" x 3"
$25

#819
Ceramic Ashtray with
Glass Bottle
Circa 1940's
4" Diameter
$100

#820
Tin Ashtray
Circa 1960's
6" x 4"
$25

#821
Plastic Ashtray
(Quincy, IL)
Circa 1970's
3" Diameter
$10

#822
Bakelite Ashtray
(Yuba City, CA)
Circa 1950's
6" Diameter
$65

#823
China Ashtray
(Indianapolis, IN)
Circa 1950's
8" Diameter
$200

#824
Ceramic Ashtray
Circa 1950's
7" x 7"
$175

SYRUP CONTAINERS

#825
Tin
Circa 1960's
One Gallon
$75

#826
Cover for Syrup Can
Circa 1940's
8" Diameter
$75

#827
Wood Barrel
Circa 1910
40 Gallon
$400

#828
Glass Jug with
Paper Label
Circa 1960's
One Gallon
$50

#829
Glass Jug with Paper Label
Circa 1910
One Gallon
$1200

#830
Paper Label
Circa 1910
24 oz.
$1500

#831
Reverse on Glass with
Metal Frame
Circa 1930's
10" x 24"
$1500

#832
Reverse Glass
(Lyons, KS)
Circa 1950's
10" x 8"
$50

#833
Tin with Glass Front
Circa 1970's
24" Diameter
$35

#834
Reverse Glass
Metal Frame
Circa 1930's
10" x 22"
$1500

#835
Reverse Glass
(Cassopolis, MI)
Circa 1950's
3 1/2" x 10"
$75

#836
Cardboard
Circa 1950's
2" x 8"
$50

#837
Tin (For Walk
In Cooler)
Circa 1940's
2" x 16"
$100

#839
Tin
Circa 1950's
12" x 28"
$125

#838
Tin
Circa 1930's
7" x 27"
$800

#840
Tin Friction (Cragstan)
with Original Box
Circa 1950's
6"
$850

#841
Plastic with Box
Circa 1940's
12"
$1100

#842
Tin Friction (Linemar)
Circa 1940's
6"
$550

#843
Tin Friction (Cragstan)
With Original Box
Circa 1950's – 11"
$1000

#844
Wooden Truck
Rubber Wheels
Circa 1930's – 24"
$850

TOYS AND GAMES

#845
Plastic Child's
Trash Can
Circa 1960's
9" x 17"
$25

#846
Nodder (Missouri
Tigers)
Circa 1960's
3" x 11"
$125

#847
Dartboard
Circa 1950's
14" x 18"
$150

#848
Paper Kite
Circa 1960's
24" x 36"
$100

#849
Paper Head Band
Circa 1950's
12" Diameter
$50

#850
Plastic Dispenser/Box
Circa 1950's
12" x 10" x 6"
$100

#851
Toy Bottle
Circa 1970's – 6"
$20

#852
Party Pak (20 Mini Btls.)
Circa 1960's
12" x 16"
$25

TOYS AND GAMES

#853
Checkerboard
Circa 1950's
14" x 14"
$150

#854
Checker Game (Wood)
Circa 1970's
14" x 14"
$75

#855
Paper Bang Gun
(Ft. Dodge, KS)
Circa 1940's
6" x 5"
$150

#856
Tin Side Piece
To Childs Toaster
Circa 1940's
5" x 3"
$75 set of two

#857
Wood and Metal
Pull Toy
Circa 1940's
10" x 9"
$650

#858
Barbie Doll with Box
Circa 1970's
12"
$25

TOYS AND GAMES

#859
Miss America Doll
Circa 1960's
20"
$300

#860
Clown Game
(Two Views)
Circa 1950's
2" Diameter
$50

#861
Stuffed Snowman
Circa 1970's
33" High
$75

#862
Plastic Billboard
For Train Set
Circa 1950's
6" x 3"
$25

#863
Golf Balls (Two Views)
Circa 1970's
1 1/2" Diameter
$10

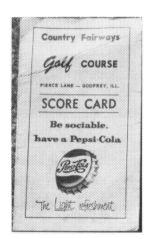

#864
Golf Scorecard
Circa 1950's
3" x 5"
$25

#865
Metal Wagon
Circa 1960's
30"
$250

TOYS AND GAMES

#866
Stuffed Santa
Circa 1970's
33" Tall
$75

#867
Stuffed Santa
Circa 1970's
26" Tall
$75

#868
Stuffed Caroler
Circa 1970's
18"
$50

#869
Stuffed Caroler
Circa 1970's
18"
$50

#870
Stuffed Caroler
Circa 1970's
18"
$50

#871
Stuffed Figure
Circa 1970's
30"
$65

TRAYS

#872
Serving Tray
Circa 1930's
14" x 11"
$850*

#873
Serving Tray
Circa 1960's
16" x 11"
$25

#874
Serving Tray
1910
11" x 14"
$2500

#875
Blue with White
Background (Tip
Tray)
1906 – 6" Diameter
$1400

#876
Serving Tray
(Mexican)
Circa 1940's
10" x 14"
$200

#877
Tip Tray (Mexican)
Circa 1960's
6" Diameter
$25

TRAYS

All Over The Map
Bigger and Better

#878
Serving Tray with
Original Box
Circa 1930's
14" x 11"
$1000

#879
Commemorative
(Zanesville, OH)
Circa 1980's
14" x 11"
$75

#880
Serving Tray
Circa 1970's
16" x 16"
$35

#881
Commemorative
(New Haven, MO)
1987 – 14" x 11"
$50

#882
Serving Tray
Circa 1950's
13" Diameter
$75

#883
Postcard (Andy Warhol
Autographed)
Circa 1970's
4" x 6"
$175

#884
Leaded Glass Shade
Circa 1970's
20" Diameter
$300

#885
Plastic Radio/Box
Circa 1960's
4" x 6"
$200

#886
Folding Chair
Circa 1950's
20" x 36"
$275

#887
Transistor Radio/Box
Circa 1960's
Box is 6" x 9"
$425

MISCELLANEOUS

#888
Cardboard Box For
Carriers
Circa 1940's
16" x 20" x 16"
$100

#889
Cardboard Box
For Crowns
Circa 1940's
50 Gross
$75

#890
Card Table
Circa 1950's
30" x 30"
$75

#891
Pencil Clip
Circa 1940's
1" Diameter
$125

#892
Wood Lid For Ingredient
Container for Pepsi Syrup
Circa 1940's – 10" Diameter
$75

#893
Clothes Brush
(Durham, NC)
Circa 1900's
7" x 3"
$200

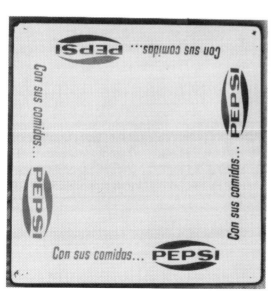

#894
Porcelain Card Table (Mexican)
Circa 1970's – 30" x 30"
$50

#895
Wood Shipping Crate
Circa 1910's – 14" x 10" x 4"
$200

MISCELLANEOUS

#896
Flashlight
Circa 1930's
3"
$75

#897
Sewing Kit
Circa 1940's
2 1/2"
$75

#898
Plastic Moneyclip
Circa 1950's
2" Diameter
$25

#899
Metal and Wood
Printblock
Circa 1940's
2" x 1"
$25

#900
Baseball Cards
Circa 1960's
4" x 6"
$15 ea.

#901
Baseball Cards
(Tulsa Oilers)
Circa 1960's
4" x 6"
$15 ea.

#902
Baseball Cards
(Tulsa Oilers)
Circa 1960's
4" x 6"
$15 ea.

#903
Tape Measure
Circa 1950's
2" x 2"
$20

#904
Tape Measure
Circa 1950's
1 1/4" x 1 1/4"
$25

#905
Glass (Etched Lettering) Coaster
Circa 1930's – 4" Diameter
$100

#906
Cardboard Coaster
Circa 1950's – 4"
$20

#907
Cardboard Coaster
Circa 1950's – 4" x 4"
$20

MISCELLANEOUS

#908
Bookmark
Circa 1940's
3" x 8"
$50

#909
Bookmark
Circa 1940's
3" x 8"
$50

#910
Bookmark
Circa 1904's
3" x 8"
$50

#911
Paper Bookmark
Circa 1940's
3" x 12"
$50

#912
Pillow
Circa 1960's
6" x 21"
$10

#913
Key Chain / ID Tag
Circa 1940's
2" x 1"
$100

#914
Calendar Holder
Circa 1950's
3" Diameter
$50

#915
Plastic Seat Cushion
Circa 1970's
13" x 13"
$25

#916
Pillow
Circa 1960's
18" Diameter
$10

MISCELLANEOUS

#917
Plastic Bottlers
Chart
Circa 1950's
3" x 10"
$50

#918
Pocket Mirror
Circa 1950's
2" Diameter
$850

#919
Scales
Circa 1950's
3'
$2500

#920
Ceramic Spoon Holder
with Original Lid
Circa 1940's
4" x 6"
$700

#921
Pocket Mirror
Circa 1900's
1 1/2" x 2 1/2"
$5500

#922
Rediclips
(Metal)
Circa
1950's
3" x 12"
$25

#923
Christmas
Tags
Circa
1950's
2" x 9"
$25

#924
Fishing Lure
Circa 1970's
3"
$10

#925
Wrapping Paper
Circa 1950's
12" x 12"
$10

#926
Bathroom Scale
Circa 1970's
14" x 10"
$15

#927
Sun Visor
Circa 1950's
12" x 12"
$35

#928
Metal Trash Can
Circa 1950's
14" x 34"
$300

#929
Token
Circa 1950's
1 1/2" Diameter
$25

#930   Blotter – Circa 1910's – 7" x 3"
$400

MISCELLANEOUS

#931
Tin Bottle Cap
(Yellow)
Circa 1930's
1" Diameter
$25

#932
Bottle Cap
Circa 1930's
1" Diameter
$25

#933
Bottle Cap
Circa 1910's
1" Diameter
$25

#934
Bottle Cap
(Dossin Food)
Circa 1940's
1" Diameter
$10

#935
Canvas Treasure Pouch
Circa 1940's
9" x 6"
$35

#936
Wooden Yo-Yo
Circa 1950's
3" Diameter
$35

#937
Reusable
Bottle Cap
Circa 1940's
1" Diameter
$75

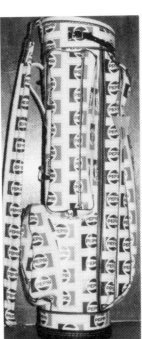

#939
Golf Bag
Circa 1970's
48"
$35

#938
Bus Ticket Folder (Two Views)
Circa 1950's
7" x 3"
$30

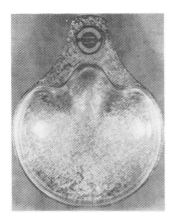

#940
Change Receiver
(Metal with Glass Insert)
Circa 1970's
6"
$25

#941
Change Receiver
(Glass)
Circa 1940's
6" x 8"
$100

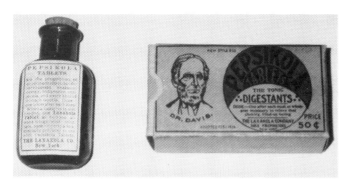

#942
Medicine Box and Bottle
(Rip Off of Pepsi Name)
Circa 1920's
4" x 2 1/2"
$25

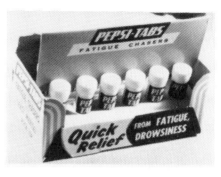

#943
Pepsi Tabs
(Rip Off of Pepsi Name)
Circa 1940's
7" x 4"
$35

#945
Paper Vendors Hat
Circa 1960's
12" x 3"
$15

#944
Change Receiver
(Mel Mac)
1968
6" x 6"
$25

#947
Change Mat (Rubber)
Circa 1960's
8" x 8"
$20

#947
Change Mat (Rubber)
Circa 1960's
8" x 8"
$20

#948
Travel Pack (Vinyl)
Circa 1950's
9" x 7"
$25

PEPSI-COLA

COLLECTIBLES

Vol. 1
(With Prices)

Pepsi-Cola collectibles are as popular as Coca-Cola items. You need this book to find the price of the item you have just purchased or are looking for. Very accurate pricing on trays to openers to jewelry to signs to coolers. Softbound, 8 1/2" x 11", B/W, 150 pages, Current Values.

Send Check or Money Order for **$14.95** + $2.00 shipping for the first book and 40¢ for each additional book to:
L-W Book Sales
P.O. Box 69
Gas City, IN 46933

Or call 1-800-777-6450 for Visa, Mastercard, and C.O.D. Orders Only!

Call (317) 674-6450 or write for FREE wholesale/retail catalog, over 600 titles of Antique Reference Books.

PEPSI-COLA

COLLECTIBLES

Vol. 2
(With Prices)

Another fine book by the experts in the Pepsi-Cola field. Completely different items found in this book than are pictured in volume one. Aprons to carriers to fans to magazine ads and many more items are pictured in this second volume of Pepsi-Cola collectibles. This book will price them for you. Softbound, 8 1/2" x 11", B/W, 192 pages, Current Values.

Send Check or Money Order for **$17.95** + $2.00 shipping for the first book and 40¢ for each additional book to:

L-W Book Sales
P.O. Box 69
Gas City, IN 46933

Or call 1-800-777-6450 for Visa, Mastercard, and C.O.D. Orders Only!

Call (317) 674-6450 or write for FREE wholesale/retail catalog, over 600 titles of Antique Reference Books.